precis

précis
1760 French noun: "cut short, condensed." [verb, 1856]

precarious
1640s legal: "held through the favor of another."
Latin: *precarius*, "obtained by asking or praying."
prex (precis): "entreaty, prayer"; "dependent on the will of another"—
the sense of "risky, dangerous, uncertain" [1680s].

pray
late 1200s: "ask earnestly, beg"; "pray to a god or saint."
Old French: *preier*.
Latin: *precari*, "ask earnestly, beg" (*prex* plural *preces precis*) "prayer, request, entreaty."
(Sanskrit) *prasna-*, "question."
(German) *fragen*, "to ask."

Related: prayed; praying, 16th century.

(a poem)

us looking up & the red glow warms the act of listening
to us, look, near & warms the speaking, to act
us, to speak in & warms, the nearing, breathing
to be in, & listen to us, look up, breathe in

listen

those

they risk language

[SIDRO]

Dead Alma ascends the blood warmred & coolants spilt across blackbright &
blue. Her body lay. Mangled multicolored. Glass at midnight.

remain limbs in those touch positions

(& her face)

vacancy & deathpluck a first verse

Aluminum flicker inside darkness.

Sustain the mood for witness.

They are
always men :

In this world, they driving Mustangs.

The sparkling scene outlines streetlights & border lights, freeway lights & reflections.
Complexity given transcendence a place always thought of. Such a small town
is Sidro.

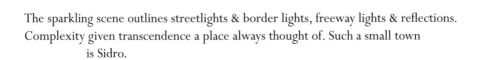

Impart

a map of memories

— the smell of brake dust is absent of faith.
This line goes —

Inside the bar evidence & facts sit leaning. There, weight against the grain. The wood
sustaining. Inside the bar reasons explain violence, are explaining, or are explanations, or
& so on

The inside of Sidro is a bar says the words. Against the body an
eighteen year old girl

                              the bar
          pushes says the words.

                              Inside
                                        locative & their forearms

              (the vinyl shoulder on the wood)

                                        [place:]
                                                   : a smalling

Guide all the world

                                say hope & glass

     to the dark

                  night inside & a collection of entreaties

collection of years after sunset. Never gray hours, never full yellow of a border morning. The end of America & this line go, & on

all the souls : imperishable undesirable kept at her side

Outside, the death of Alma is recorded into the digital space shaking in some hand — some fingers fumble at the edges between — will be print, anyway & a generality. Of simple. Tomorrow. Front doors & drive ways, neatly folded:

Too many Almas in Sidro the paper reads *city can't rid them fast enough*

to create the room, empty the buildings, disoccupy the seats, the buses, the lines. The letters of history kept busied in the small town of Sidro ensure the progress. The death of Alma Gonzalez breaks the backs. All the little black letters free from their natural inclination to stasis. Little letters remain the fragments of her body. A Santo is free.

The rain of her death back to the sudden earth is a fivehundred year explosion. The boulevard ends at a pier leading into the center of a reflecting Pacific. Silver suddenly, vomiting head into sea. The night holds little fragments & spreads it like sky *like bread for everyone* whispers Alma. Like death. *For everyone* purrs the motor of a white Ford Mustang corralled in tape, fed shards of glass by gloved officers, & cutlets of hair & denim like straws of hay by the awed tourists of this country.

Like bread, bodies are for everyone.
The border is an old scar that continues to live, a thick fold
where bushes gather & lights metal. Dirt there
made yellow fades blue to the north, fades blue to the south.
A scar leaks out into the ocean. Along the water is bright from sand

along the sand is dark from earth. Along the whorl,
lights blink in rhythm to a small city named Sidro.

Along the scar always walking
an act creased into the duty,
always a rhythm, & the rhythm is duty.

All those, as sleep, breathe in community, a night that continues anyway
breathing, & is breath the voice of the dreamt breathing,
& is dreamt now, something to be recorded.

The story begins.
History, like bread, is for Everyone explains Alma to her own body
lay below where it has been
tucked into eternity
& misspelled.
A speeding, drunken car in Sidro

car hits girl in Sidro; 1 dead, driver arrested

A 17-year old girl was killed instantly and a 5-year-old girl she was with was injured late Saturday night when they were struck by a car while trying to cross Palm Ave in the South Bay neighborhood of Nestor.

Police said the girls were crossing the street, in violation of no-crossing or jay walking signs, at 11:18 pm when they were hit by a west bound Ford Mustang. The driver was later arrested on suspicion of drunk driving.

The dead girl was identified as Alma Gonzales of Sidro. The younger girl, whose identity was not released, is expected to survive. Police said she suffered a fractured pelvis and numerous cuts and scrapes.

The driver was identified as Roger Ramsay, 41.

The accident happened west of Interstate 5 in a section of Palm Ave filled with bars, dance clubs and markets.

Because the girls were at fault in the accident, Ramsay was charged only with driving while under the influence of alcohol, San Diego Police said.

EDITORIAL NOTE

The awareness of aboriginal tongues touches upon in aural América, the critical significance of possibly being able to explain the particular agonistic evolutions within the ["to lay upon"; "place, put"; "into, in"] of el castellano within distinct countries of the Continent.

In the Central American region, two notable indigenous tongues exercised a marked influence over Language: Maya & those diverse dialects/ tongues of Nahua. The first was spoken in the Mexican southeast, northeastern Guatemala, southeastern Honduras & in some regions of Nicaragua. The dialects of Nahua dispersed through the entire Mexican antiplano & along the meridinal coast, from the actual coast of Sinaloa to the Republic of Costa Rica.

The dialect spoken in Tenochtitlán during the arrival of Cortés were those ending in "tl" & were spread by Aztec conquistadors throughout those areas owned & operated by them. Eased by bureaucracy in place, the Spaniards converted it into a [   ] lingua franca, which served understanding between all the towns of New Spain.

Along the Pacifica coastline, dialects ending in "t" were spoken; in Guatemala & El Salvador, those being called nahuat or pipil.

The profound acculturation ("to bear, endure"; "to carry" as with, diaspora & nation] by the indigenous nuclei of El Salvador has forced an almost complete disappearance of nahuat as tongue speak–

NOTA EDITORIAL

El conocimiento de las lenguas aborígenes reviste en nuestra América una gran importancia, ya que sin tal conocimiento no nos es posible entender y explicar las particulares evoluciones sufridas por el castellano en los distintos países del Continente.

En el área centroamericana, dos notables lenguas indígenas ejercieron marcada influencia sobre el idioma de los conquistadores: el maya y los diversos dialectos de la lengua nahua. La primera se hablaba en el sureste mexicano, noreste de Guatemala, suroeste de Honduras y en algunas regiones de Nicaragua. Los dialectos nahuas se extendían por todo el altiplano de México y la costa meridional, desde el actual Estado de Sinaloa hasta la República de Costa Rica. .

El dialecto hablado en Tenochtitlán a la llegada de Cortés, era de los terminados en "tl" y había sido difundido por los aztecas en las regiones conquistadas por ellos. Debido a esto los españoles lo convirtieron en una verdadera lingua franca, de la cual se sirvieron para entenderse con todos los pueblos de la Nueva España.

A lo largo de la costa del Pacífico se hablaban dialectos terminados en "t", siendo el de Guatemala y El Salvador el llamado nahuat o pipil.

La profunda aculturación sufrida por los núcleos indígenas de El Salvador ha hecho que el nahuat casi desaparezca como lengua habla-

El Nawat de Cuscatlán, Pedro Geoffroy Rivas. 1969 por Ministerio de Educación, Dirección General de Cultura.

[crossing/fantasy]

laces
yellow from dust, the sun
sinks   black at dusk
mountains shadows sway

soon dissolution
nightscape come

scrape tips the plastic
laces
scratch echo they laugh
Dolores

to stare
wiggle lips

laugh

rage to surrender

no one
Her wonder
wander them
hang a loop

under

a sharp finger sticks out
& always a hole the size of
anger

no one
wonders

—

In the aluminum
sheet
rusted to borderfence
stretch
               gone be
               A fence
to no one

under
No one else will
watch
grow dark

The color

Laces

Rustdecay

the rich of
no
          one
Her eyes make faint
laces sand frame hole

Reflections from the lastlight
         & a kind of
                 lake

[: the family law system]

Hers & the faces of men who handled little bodies sheathed in scales.

all crossing while crossing city fast & solid   try as she might to remember
the soft endsand & the continuesong pass from fading waves to breezes she can't
hold to it. Cars seconds round : a watch & calendar, a city named Tijuana

architecture   being

movement

Movement : History found

Tijuana in both
& by nightfall conceived Amnesia y América (how far in history do forgotten
                                                    marks

    &
    The morning collects its papers
Movement to History return
        their work (how far in America does forgetting

                                    / forget

America the lullabies/ the broken strain of memory

    with songs of stolen & captive people

[nation building / women's legal identity : —————————]

This is such a book:

In 2006 former governor of California Pete Wilson was invited by the Hudson Institute to discuss proposition 187 and California's struggle with immigration in general. In the talk, titled by Wilson "Illegal Immigration: Past, Present, and Future," the former governor makes constant appeals to two pathological axes of American historical consciousness. One is the rule of law. The other is citizen children, his term used to describe children born to immigrant mothers in North Amer-

From Veracruz, outside Veracruz on a street running directly westward into the country from the ocean, she made the long walk to Jalapa whispering the same son about a highway. In Jalapa she visited her mother's grave & stole a horse from her brother. As she rode past him & then away from him she whispered again to the horse. Then to the men in corridors & walkways.

Await the morning call. Sleep towards the pull of the long walk away from dreams. A reality of work & songs & walking to be sung: the sea, the highway & goodbyes.

The horse died as she remembered an even older traditional son about Jalapa & the sanctuary provided by a southern horizon awoken, laid a restful elegy over the horse's body. Movement on the highway alone or static. Movement whispering circular sons, simply hear the whispersong. Close, the terror of loudness & repetitive melody of goodbye & Jalapa, highway & horizon. Movement, scoop her from the bloated grave. The old son looped in small dust devils, movement-move again, north again.

San Luis Potosí: buses & buses, cities & highways. Movement to Tijuana was like remembering old traditional songs in the place where they were born amidst the things that inspired them to be written, sung the way they were sung. Risk the loudness of their singing. Locate this precisely. Son is a melody repeated twice, by two, by one until another is remembered by looking out into horizons blooming over cities past. Sing with me.

ica, and thus aligning National temporality to the legal identity of women as bearers of future citizens; women, that is, not as beings but machinery. The coming together of these discourses reveals the heteropatriarchy at work in the opinions against imigrants, particularly women – that they bear a potential to unravel the structural empiricisms of cultural identity: body, place, language,

Close her eyes in van.

She: imagine the city outside
piece to gather from a book read so far.

This set out amidst
nothingness, desert patrolled at little
hours,
voices controlled at all times. From
silence
the crossing begins.

Imagine it small enough to see at the end.

From the practice of lullabying a small girl to sleep in a small
port town in Veracruz & the habit of breathing in & out old
sons, writing, the over active habit of transcribing visible
reality to melodies easily repeating, she starts her last walking,
the desert closely holding inside her mind & the phenomena in
the lyric sung cannot remove the marking of things left behind
—

and memory.

Señora. Señora, hay que movernos. Apúrese, señora, ya viene la mañana.

Mís tenis.

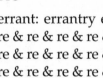

BIO

errant: errantry err *itarere* ere re
re & re & re & re & re & re & re &
re & re & re & re & re & re & re &
re & re & re & re & re & re & re &
re & re & re & re & re & re & re &
re & re & re & re & re & re & re &

[dismantling composition]

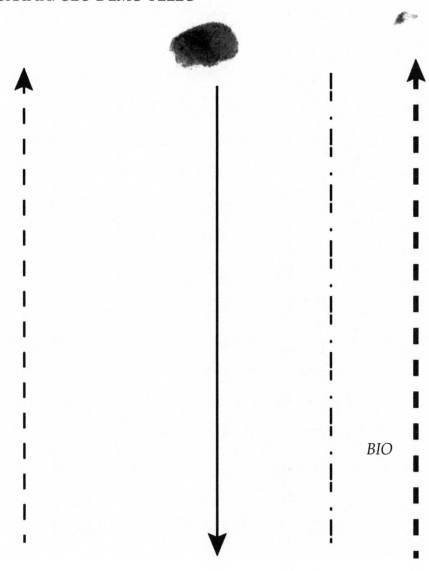

GRAFIA: GEO DEMO TELEO

BIO

The rule of law is used to encode "obedience" within modes of self-management ascribed to certain beings. In the case of law's assemblage of place, construed in Wilson's sense of time ["past, present, and future"] "obedience" is the temporal life of those subject categories that intersect around questions of power and neglect, of exclusion, enforcement, and (im)mobilities codified by the border politicized in arrangements force and nationalism.

City is
an organ the body
ocean

feeling

swaying bag

hanging
bodying knees
bending calculating
distancing

streets measure pacing.

Women's bodies are de/com-
posed and managed, integrated.
Their wombs are captivated by
Shoelaces hang through a holing of a Nation, religion,
& an aluminum fence. given to one moral law, biopoli-
tics are enforced as necropolitics.
The manifestation of temporali-
Laces withouting, shoes sway. ty, of power articulates this legal
authority in the practices of
border policing and is embodied
in Wilson's speech :

A light breeze crawls along the breadloaf grooves.

Aluminum sheet spreads horizontal, canals.
Thought stops her.

white strings
held together   a knot she tied

A horizon unravels elegy above
lain down.

She only breathes
to continuewalk.

crosses left
are prints left afterwards by birdfeet

smell of little things
sounds of wings   of insects

see
circles rebound

moving dark scattering

desert light frequent
eight open graves

decision to sit
                    a blank name on the lips

pronounce the air pronoun even
scatters night &
the position

the smellmirrors & corpsehair is

a metaphor: *spiderwebs*, the world dries over

all the characters named will soon walk into themselves
the ocean receives wash in the surf

quote And by that time you'll have had children – *citizen children*. And that, my friends, is how we will get

in those fields to 20, 35, 50 million – unless earlier we reach a point of such moral fatigue that we no longer even pretend to enforce our immigration laws. We repeal them, disband the border patrol, and have open borders. Long before that day comes, America will no longer be the country that attracted those

ants driven to chaos dances from the feet sound sharp stones. Vowels dissipate. Break apart hard dirt rocks. Consonants retaliate. The lingering murmur of the truck long down the road. Capital nominates. Lights look back. Fall. Marks. Back.

Back.

With her mother to beach, the sky. The sky, then reddening the humidity. Marking weighing heavy on the branches. Thin progress in trees casting shadows. The beach at that hour gray & littered. Broken shells colored pale bone burnt of wood. The look of paper scraps tallied fish scratched. Ink & marks, fly back stay. Fall black. Hammer an echo. Fishman voice & the drum wood. The drum wood & the boat wood. Thin trees. Fat radio fire & the fish talk, the man voice. Sung songs in Fishanman fishman dialect voice. White crumpled insects over the sand again. Gusts against her feet & through yellow plastic sandals. The hour waits for fish & man. Her small feet little ducks beside the fat toes of her mom. Toes turned into walking : the sand like jelly stuck to the insides again.

a Memory like that need:

mother's face as waves came in. The face a seeing, sees the first time, the world mimes the noise closest a heartbeat. Close eyes halfmouth & tongueshy. Behind lips taste salt & flake skind fishskin hands of men. Fingers in the pound an off shore breeze again. A face through hair. Rhythm does again. The poet wave. Poem traces again.

generations of legal immigrations who im-
only the fishandman & the mark of again
migrated under the rule of law. **end quote** The focus on taxes in Wilson's political-theoretical framework is legitimated
memory is again re- an "er" of stutter:
by an unspoken construct: that of the woman as "birth-mother." The mother's role in this nation-building imaginary isn't that of raising children, but rather of yielding children to the set of morals and history that builds citizens, the Nation. Thus, taxes come to represent what is not addressed: all children are adopted, and national personhood normed to paternal-maternal fantasy.

In this arrangement of exchanges immigrant women are doubly alienated by the precarious status of their bodies as producers of assembled bodies, potential persons, producers of inferior citizens. The normal exchange of material subsistence cannot account for the innate deficit of these bodies with an inherent, biological, conceived origin in a "peripheral," "Third World" country :

Where are my men again. Why a little girl written again: the sky is only red humidity

A mark.

quote You have got this long, porous border. You have got this nation full of people, poor people. It is full of poor people. It is not a poor country in terms of resources, but it is full of poor people. **end quote**

Never find a way back sand.

One other.

Drucilla Cornell asserts, "the obsession with genetic ties is also tied into unconscious fantasies about the meaning of masculinity and racial superiority." Fantasies are stories, descriptions of an inconsistent universe, one with a different tempo, cadence, like Wilson's temporality; his past is not actual, the present is not a full one, and the future is a fantastical arrangement that preserves modes of exchange, assembles flesh,

Nation of language

is a thought.

and keeps patriarchy em-powered.
Stories are temporal, locative, and
dismantling. Place written as time
in-place. Border stories focus on
women or the young, the young re-
membering between two national

Es mejor que pase la lluvia.

matrices – that of their birth, that
of their adoption. This story is both
true and fantasy, a truth within the
patriarchy-fantasy, and a fantasy
rehearsed to undo a truth about the
place of women in-place, a writing
cadence from the border.

[*]

---

*The San Diego Union Tribune, 1998 - 2002

Man's body washes ashore near border

Border Field State Park - Authorities are trying to determine what killed a man whose body washed ashore at the park early Thursday.

The county Medical Examiner's Office had not identified the body, said to be that of a Latino male. The death was not believed to be a homicide, the Sheriff's Department said.

Heavy surf washed the body onto the beach at the park just north of the US-Mexican border about 7 a.m. Thursday, the Sheriff's Department said.

Man's body found in Sidro field

Sidro – San Diego police are investigating the death of a man whose body was found in a field yesterday morning near a community center on Sycamore Road.

Police said the death was suspicious, but said the unidentified man may have died from a drug overdose and then been dragged to a nearby field. An autopsy will be performed.

Need for minority prep courses cited

The low representation of Latinos and African Americans in the University system can be attributed to a lack of access to college preparatory courses while in high school, experts who testified at a state hearing here said yesterday.

Only four percent of Latinos and three percent of African Americans who graduate from high school are eligible to apply for the University.

The state's Master Plan for Education recommends that the state ensure that all students have access to an academically rigorous curriculum.

Army attempt to recruit upsets Tijuana

Tijuana- A US Army Sergeant's attempt to recruit students from a Tijuana public school has developed into a maelstrom over Mexican sovereignty and US recruiting practices.

The San Diego County based recruiter, identified by Mexican officials as Sgt. Jorge Castro, visited a Tijuana college preparatory school last week, where he asked permission to talk to students about the military's educational opportunities.

Some Mexicans qualify for the US military because they were born in the United States or have legal status from living there temporarily.

A crack begins as a precursor to rain.

— :

as if to say speech acts
as if to say sonorously to
contemplate, language in time   to keep euphony   to hear dissonance
in dissent & a time-space   thin reeds to keep, relate to in   towards two lips,
sustain/a breath, love   a moment/breath
        provide prose
in precise   as if to keep active   precis poetry   measured
from
praecis cut from also mine

        this matter/of fraction & space   the origin resonates is
expanding   is world sing   silence knot binary to sounds

        historic tongue make says   meant as/excavate lips to
                tremors, the reeds hidden over the field in my memory
            produce turning the poem/ turning story by culture & diaspora
firstly   silence/withhold silence &
writing/act, the voice of silence/loss

            translate place-sound
            weight language the speaking of allows   yes
        permiss sediment/state of permit permitee   permiter ere
eres tú
                    word is that?

inceptual than signifying   sonorous than saying   wordseek
omission/refusals after ininside   the trial of carrying out experience, the
present permit,   the excavation of is-always   presentthis   move-
mentfield
energy/compositionsilent potentialis hum   a knowledge as if to impart
condition

The maps of modernity may ask:

To which silence responds

in places

we choose & don't

this way

what we don't know becomes force our tongues search

sound for a meaning

[cartograph]

: that something that is below

the grass will swallow it

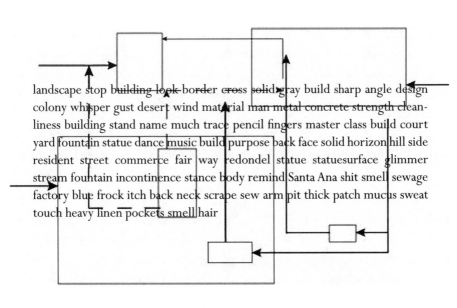

landscape stop building look border cross solid gray build sharp angle design colony whisper gust desert wind material man metal concrete strength cleanliness building stand name much trace pencil fingers master class build court yard fountain statue dance music build purpose back face solid horizon hill side resident street commerce fair way redondel statue statuesurface glimmer stream fountain incontinence stance body remind Santa Ana shit smell sewage factory blue frock itch back neck scrape sew arm pit thick patch mucus sweat touch heavy linen pockets smell hair

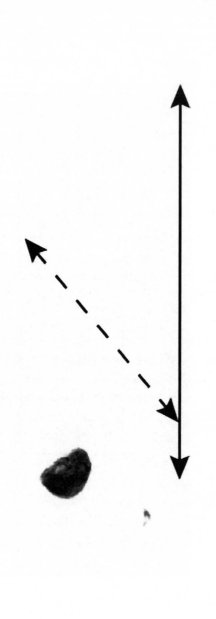

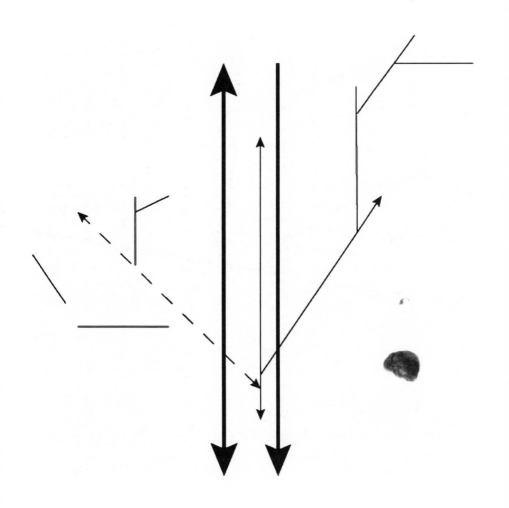

1.5 Auxiliary Verbs.

a) The verbs "ser" & "estar" do not exist, which are overemphasized in grammatical constructions. For example, if one says istaxucit', one means to say "flor blanca." If one says ne xucit' istak, one is saying "la flor (is) blanca."

b) Generally, the verb "live" nemi, is used to indicate "being":

ken ti-nemi?: "how do you live, how is your being?"

se siwatihlan iwan se ukictihlan nem tik ne culal: "a hen and a rooster live (are being) in the coop."

Other verbs that carry auxiliary functions are welia, "will to _____"; neki, "will to want to will _____," yawi, "will to want to go _____" & wiz, "will to want to will myself to you, where you are, so we may be there & between us & our willing to be there together, Be here."*

1.5 Verbos auxiliarees

a) No exísten los verbos 'ser' y 'estar', los cuales se sobreentiende en las construcciones gramaticales. Si se dice, por ejemplo, istaxucit', se quiere significar 'flor blanca'. Si se dice ne xucit' istak, se está diciendo 'la flor (es) blanca'.

b) Generalmente se usa el verbo 'vivir' nemi, para indicar 'estar':

ken ti-nemi?: 'cómo vives, cómo estás?'

se siwatihlan iwan se ikictihlan nem tik ne culal, 'una gallina y un gallo viven (están) en el corral'.

Otros verbos que desempeñan funciones auxiliares son welia, 'poder'; neki, 'querer', yawi, 'ir' y wizi, 'venir'

*El Nawat de Cuscatlán, Pedro Geoffroy Rivas. 1969, por Ministerio de Educación, Dir. General de Cultura

The San Diego Union-Tribune, ... January 31, 2003

Immigrants testify of fatal crash

Border Patrol was pursuing pickup

By Susan Gembrowski
STAFF WRITER

...corded a... to Tecate.
They then wal ed with a dozen others, climbing a fence at the border, and were accom anied by Moreno, 20, and Pedroza, 20.

...for his life when the pickup ...ed towar him as he dove ...f the the st on Old Highway 80.

Driver is for Moreno and...

...ther at the Border Patrol. Two at the scene and a third died of his injuries at a hospital.

...ther public debate about illegal immigration...

...hind.

A 17-year-old woman, who died in the crash, was riding in the back right se of the pickup. The illegal immigrants were th ose front the vehicle when th crashed on a bridge abutment a west of 18 near home of the Border Patrol.

Ana Lewis one that was found under
...detailing a under.

...N ... E. Lewis
/ Union-Tribune

Fatal journey from border

Crash of fleeing pickup left 3 immigrants dead

By Alex Roth
STAFF WRITER

EL CAJON —

...traveled ye ...begins with the sea ... at Tecate ... of earlier that ...killed three people.

They said... group as and walked seve al mile where four of them cro and the rest were herd truck, covered with a ta their hide n down.

The p... eventually abutment, overthrown...

...one ...ering. He is ...abutment on

...ther reading statements.
"T stifying through an interpret r, one of the passengers, ...g...ez, ..., gff, who is from Durango, Mexico, said that t o days before the Jan. 9 crash he had traveled to Tijuana, where he met a smuggler who told him to board a bus to Tecate.

At Tecate he ... storms and Pedroza, who he said promised to smuggle him into the United States in e changed for a payment of $1,500 after e

13 passengers were charged $1,500 each

...group, re aimed ...the border and re ched the pickup — walk that nated about 90 to 45 minutes... once they crossed into the nited States — Gonzalez and 12 other passengers were told to lie in the bed of the pickup, wi a tarp, he said.

The tr k began to move and at some point Tretcos became ... ... but a Border Patrol was pu sate the pickup. The pickup beg to pick up with its motor. at points in pursuit and a believe... head, he said.

The pursuit lasted about 10 to 15 minutes, with one of the pickup's tires "blowing out at one point, soon after an ry over a spot strip issued by the Border Patrol.

Then came the crash. Tretcos said he suffered head wounds and was treated at a...

...three were killed. Some are being held as material witnesses, some are being held by immigration officials and some are free after posting a bond with immigration authorities.

At least two of the illegal immigrants were treated at hospitals and then vanished before the Border Patrol could take them into custody, according to Pedroza's attorney, Barton Sheela.

The hearing is scheduled to continue tomorrow before Superior Court Judge Patricia Cookson.

[*Eutiquia*]

remembersound

Rememberingthesound Rememberthesound Remembersound Rememberthesound Rememberthesound
Remember the
sound made
        by walking through bodies. Remember
        the crossing -
                There are ghosts there.

Walk simple. Food & feeding. Shitting without a finger up your ass.
Hooked
small shovel or hoe scrape it out
messily
pull smears across useless muscles
        a disconnected rectum. Rectum cut
        from brain, spinal chord
        then no longer & definition.

A broken neck. Metal bars sprout from the skin.
Metal bars sprout from sand. Metal bars sprout long along a road,
        lights hang from heads drop
        sweat hold in the sun. One broken windshield.
        Smell of brake dust & warm oil at midnight.

A soft cloud of smoke like milk.   — say, man/ [say]
American.
Van an egg & the bodies what. Shimmering useless warmth man say,
América.

Metal bars
in line with neck hold machine where
many machines there are only machines.

Alma traces them with her finger as she sits on top of head, her delicate head. (let's imagine
this in this attempt to imagine the same hurt.) She traces the tubes & the lights, them…
Door is a window, window is a window. Everyone open. Everyone works to keep machines
breath: :ing. Alma — breathe hears voice like the breathing. A city at night. The breathing of.
Cloud holding in. Everyone asking. Everyone *precising*.

        — knows the strength of cars. Their wheels do not stop. They will push through you.

The thin metal rods sticking out of head look like a crown.
Rods all through small body.
          must be in her forties. Her body
          small & light.

Easy for a joke about body. Or the cynicism. All that vulnerability alongside her skin
exposed to the community laugh.

Immortality of memory as something that could be said & would you regret it always.

It is being that is fragile & vulnerable.   It is [   ] that looked into a
        sky with /momented/ us.   [that is, in the moment of it —]

                Say her name America

NO MORE DEATHS IN THE DESERT

Once again the temperatures in the desert have broken the 100-degree mark. & once again, the number of immigrants dying while trying to cross that desert into the United States is reaching unprecedented numbers *Por favor ciuda|d|*   *|r|*   recuérdame. *Por favor no me dejen morir sin* n|h|*ombre, sin que sepan los demás que siguen mi camino.* That is why a group of activists decided to retrace the ███████████, ██████████████████ plight of immigrants & demand changes in US immigration laws.

The group is called "No More Deaths." Members are people fro███████████████████████████████rts of the country
███████████████████████████████████ stop the deaths of immigrants

I see   halt belts that wrap arou
          e abandoned cars left behind
              nside them already dead or
                  es. I   *about these bo*
                      d the deaths on those parts
                        e always   *to*
myself.
   dust, quickly   *my skin*
     uia Cortés was in one of   *th*
       ight. I remember   *her*
        he fell on me &I   *felt her spine break.*
          osquito in   *the palm of you*
            even   *though most, I*

As the activists walked through the desert *Me
llamo Eutiquia Cortés. Tengo un hijo. Soy de El Salvador.
Trabajé en Tijuana para el dinero de la crusada. Soñaba con
████████████████████████*, the Border Control initiative
was kicking into full gear. The $10 billion program
includes the ██████ █████manned aerial vehicles, helicopters,
fixed wing ███████████more than 200 additio███ Border
Patrol agents to increase border surveillance.

   The goal is to████████████████████████████l
the consequences could be deadly for immigrants who are
not

   A coyote will   anywhere

       Th
ir helicopters
     he hotter mon
        in the place of my
               send invisible si
               suffocate in
                     ere   digs al
                     erson helps me.

The summer months are without a doubt the most
treacherous. Temperatures rise to 125 degrees. It is during
these months that immigration increases due to more work
opportunities in the fields. But it is also during this time
that more immigrants find death instead of work.

   A family of eight dead, a baby still feeding off its
dead mother's ████████████████████████████████████

       will open my eyes, & if it is true, if my spine does

not work, then I will walk the command myself across my body & across my scars & these pins.

                the worst of this. I have walked three

       the car that failed me,   *to my eyes, I*

    myself. & once I have

walk some more, to my hands, to my mouth, to my lungs & there I will take my hands

                  once I am

to my toes. I   *already, now I*

    for the

real & if that is what turns out to have been

       e it.

             a woman who paid a coyote to take her sister over the border. A few days later, she got a call ████████████████████████████ not have to pay. Her sister had a broken leg & would be left stranded.   her sister's decomposed body ████ able to identify her by a ring she had given her when she turned fifteen. ████████████████████████

████████████████ eliminate the militarization of the border

[red]

The red gone behind what spreads
itself a cross : the like : a sky : is metal is mauve
pulled behind the pacific still immense
that hour thin blanket
dying heatpush last smell : slaves
smog & sewage hangborn to
lapping waves across estuaries' silt
& fields : Sidro. What's heard   they crawl
the low bushes   gusts
creep crackboard fence privatespace in
property line   gaze fond framed moment
home before being   pull dark   page sky atom
sink rainbow bellied fish   slip
hands of deep & deeper
unfamiliar eyes substance water. Smells of a day
that Sidro smells   day.

Settle under hand the evening
turn & turn versecold & dark   purple.
Cloudfloat through
watch ocean dark standface
the blind
whisper declare waves with out
wordmake any thing more.

Poems of the day settle
recitation
all two-words
far Sidro
a color falling in moments.

some more blue or root a line a poem
finger tracing some thing imagined
folds

this moment & when the sky is
compare   Sidro
it happens   outside

If there is no labor there is no
labor.

Tierra sin nombre, sin América,
estambre equinoccial, lanza de púrpura,
tu aroma me trepó por las raíces
hasta la copa que bebía, hasta la más delgada
palabra aún no nacida de mi boca. *

If there is no development there is no development.

* Pablo Neruda, *Canto General*.

SHOUT

               remember

                             in

                                      sound

                                                    -ing

language

What would it sound like if not like a machine

    your breath erasing breath

the dark clouds in the distance where we suspect the rain to hide
the breath you felt come from inside you,
the breath you witnessed erase
                             moves
                 away
           stands at the opposite end of this field
                    foreign
             staring
         back at you...

...is no longer yours. You learn that it never was.

        tongue has always waited
your eyes
in what you believe &
        the things you have truly succeeded
falling towards the earth...

You become lost inside the earth amongst the rest, the sun bright on the grain & living

give form to what you've lost.

What's your name?

What's my name?
Give me a name.

…always so demanding.

I'm always so demanding.

Only one name

Whose?

In English.

What is a ghost?

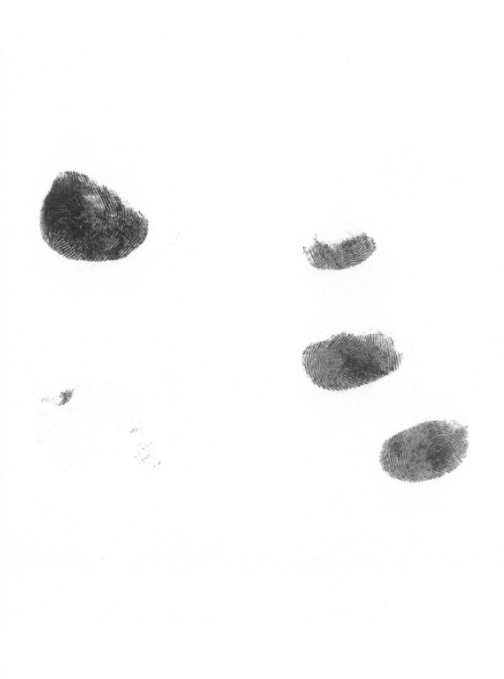

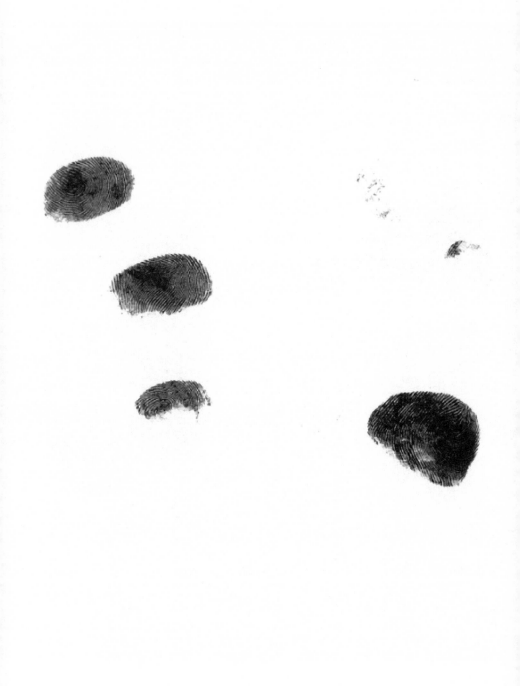

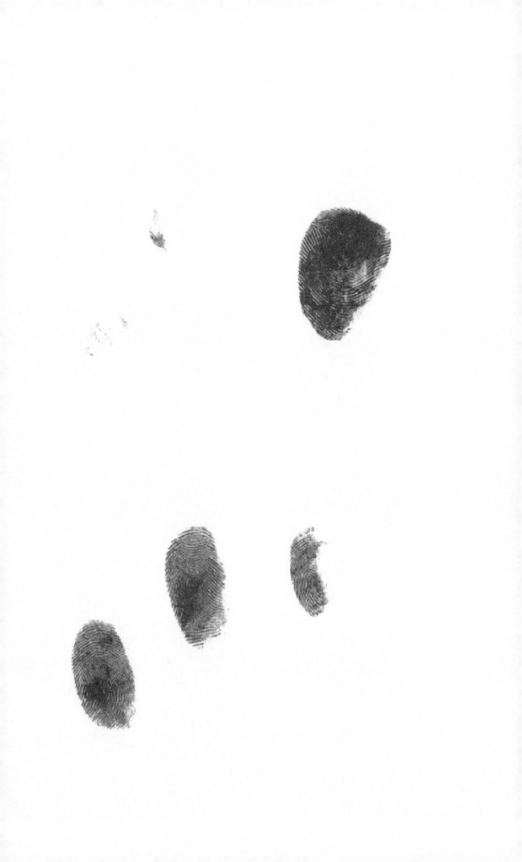

this whole time

précis : **epilogue**

To approach words from poetry is a form of asking questions.

La distancia entre una palabra y su significado es el espacio de la transformación.

— Cecilia Vicuña

And so it goes until the vista includes only displacement of feeling back into the body, which gave birth to the feelings that don't sit comfortably inside the communal. — Claudia Rankine, *Citizen: An American Lyric*

The Tijuana River Valley opens to the Pacific porously. A wide estuary, unimaginable as inhabitable though habitat — overly imaged, uncommonly mapped as the US/Mexico Border.

Palm Ave. connects Imperial Beach to the 5. It's a long broad avenue, vibrant, diverse between old and new commerce. On either side are residential zones. I grew up in Nestor. Nestor is situated between Imperial Beach, San Ysidro, and the estuary. I lived there for nearly eighteen-years, roughly the age of Alma Gonzalez, who died crossing Palm Ave. when she and a friend were run over by a drunk driver. The driver was never charged for her death. The day after her death less than 200 words in the San Diego Union Tribune explained that

————————————the girls were crossing the street, in violation of no-crossing or jay walking signs, at 11:18 pm when they were hit by a west bound Ford Mustang. The driver was later arrested on suspicion of drunk driving.

The driver was identified as Roger Ramsay, 41.

The accident happened west of Interstate 5 in a section of Palm Ave filled with bars, dance clubs and markets.

The place filled with bars and clubs and markets is
not inhabitable. It is imageable. It is mappable to the
visitor, the pilgrim.

precis came into form in trying to make sense of what
is or is made not habitable. Sometimes the reason is called
violence. Sometimes it remains simply implacable. To
think of violence and a history of the Americas, for
example, is to begin with the war between Iberian
imperialism securing a new habitability by re-assem-
bling indigenous habitability. One national expansion
violently imposes itself on the territories of existing
nations. Then the moment arrives when the violence
of then is the methodology of now. That is, history
and its intrinsic power to make Nature and to make
Society, is deciphered in the academic terminologies
of time and governments, modern, postmodern, and
so on.

Alma was posthumously found guilty of jaywalking,
not dying, but responsible for her own precarity, her
own corporeal difference to the hard and fast surface
of a Mustang, and a driver who was drunk. But that drunken-
ness remains decriminalized by measuring culpability
between jaywalking and drunk-driving, expendabili-
ty, culpability, criminality. What place is habitable
(where was he in such a rush to?)

Post-1492, what the uninhabitable tells us, then, is that populations who
occupy the "nonexistent" are living in what has been previously conceptu-
alized as the unlivable and unimaginable. ...identity and place are
mutually constructed, the uninhabitable spatializes a human Other
category of the unimaginable — Catherine McKittrick, *Demonic Grounds*

**A vertical-to-horizontal shift in how power is being experienced and
understood charges human relations with a strange, perverse, new
shimmer of "equality," which results in ever-new methods of democrat-
ically exchanged hostilities. — Chela Sandoval,** *Methodology of the Oppressed*

And not habitable, (wherein must've Alma's body found itself so suddenly to be, simply and informally, flesh?) — I cannot rely on the narratives that exist because they operate in-general. The causality (or morality) of expansion, the law* (or uninhabitability) of territory, the grace (or tax) of imposition.

The Southwesternmost Borderfield Memorial Park is the geographic focus of Gloria Anzaldúa's opening poem to the chapter "The Homeland Aztlán: El otro México." It has been made real to the academics and her readers as the barbed wire, the "the edge where earth touches ocean/ where the two overlap/ a gentle coming together/ at other times and places a violent clash."

1994 Operation Gatekeeper
1994 Proposition 187
1994 Proposition 184
1996 Proposition 209
1998 Proposition 227
2000 Proposition 21
2000 Proposition 22

---

*In California, the ballot initiative process allows citizens to change laws directly by majority vote without going through legislative representatives. Touted as "direct democracy," California ballot campaigns require large amounts of funding as well as legal counsel. Most propositions on the ballots are drafted primarily by wealthy citizens and politicians, and many are aimed either at expanding state powers in order to police marginalized populations or at decreasing state resources that help the same aggrieved groups. This is a central contradiction of neoliberalism. As social services and health care are cut more of people's incomes have to cover the costs of an always-shrinking social safety net, even as hourly wages and employee benefits remain stagnant at best. For impoverished and legally vulnerable populations, these conditions essentially make welfare necessary, but those who need it are denigrated as eschewing their "personal responsibility" to care for themselves and their families. — Lisa Marie Cacho, *Social Death*

Looking west from the mesas east of the primary port of entry at San Ysidro, the Otay mesas, looking west towards the place where Anzaldúa's feet sink into the sand, the valley is a soft brush of grey and blue hues. At dusk the marine layer gorges on fractals of light and the red includes the border's truth and its experiences, the "feelings" as Rankine writes, "that don't sit comfortably." *precis* looks for the communal. The distinctions between the overlapping gentle coming togethers and where violence clashes. The feelings locked in the silence of the sight where there is no national language yet to release their claims, arguments, or histories. Where "disruptions of discourse" discourse (*disruptions* as M. NourbeSe Philip has put it in describing hemisphere).

The project of *precis* is a project of nation language, to borrow the Barbadian poet Kamau Brathwaite's term and practice (of a postnational speech act), and to continue with Anzaldúa's geographic project of mapping the place of borders in the US through the play of different languages, their structures and usages, their expenditure into the verifiability of both experience and truth. *precis* started as an attempt to put into knowledge and to put into words, to fit into a form that would sit comfortably, the death of Alma Gonzalez. The short newspaper clipping I have kept since her death reveals to me a large and uncomfortable distance between the ways of memorializing the person, Alma, of condemning the time in San Diego where reporting on death in the area engulfed in that beautiful and soft hue of marine layer was made simple (to make formal the imposition), and of creating something worth the value of her lifehood without it being contingent on the so called facts of her general life. Mapped so conclusively already by the image of the border. *precis* is a project in making maps. Giving form to language, meaning to forms.

This art is practiced on and over the edge of politics, beneath its ground, in animative and improvisatory decomposition of its inert body. It emerges as an ensemblic stand, a kinetic set of positions, but also takes the form of embodied notation, study, score. Its encoded noise is hidden in plain sight from the ones who refuse to see and hear—even while placing under constant surveillance — the thing whose repressive imitation they call for and are. — Fred Moten and Stefano Harney, *The Undercommons*

Rather than lyricize or historicize violence in the Americas, the hemisphere, or a transnationally conceptualized border, let porousness be the palpable atmosphere, the red sky when it is also a place, a site of formal being. The palpable atmosphere of affinity comes in and out of the grasp of a form to which it fits comfortably. Not the grasp of language, which is itself always the ecology of comprehending enunciations. *precis* lets form seep in and between, and out through the porousness of what settles to the page.

The strength of the neo-liberal ideology, on a popular level, is its emphasis on individual liberty, freedom and personal responsibility. Those have all been very important aspects, of what you might call 'American Ideology' since the very inception of what the U.S. has been about. What neo-liberalism did was to take the demand for that which was clearly there in the 1950's and the 1960's and say "We can satisfy this demand, but we are gonna do this a certain way, we are gonna do it through the market, and you can only achieve those goals through the market. We are gonna do it in such a way that you have to forget about the issues of social justice." — David Harvey, on the New Imperialism, in *Logos* 5.1, 2006

The market-state-logic is a fragile balance that requires the establishment of formal modes of citizen-participation. The effects of this reverberate throughout the transnational hemisphere as demands on labor and natural resource, and, significantly, dispossess persons from within previous markets, imposing the necessity for migration to solve the financial dismantling of those once stable social realities. What becomes the "border fantasy" is the coupling of personal responsibility, freedom, and accumulation-by-dispossession. Immigrant "stories" are either valorized for the personal responsibility of work ethic and the achievement of American consumer-citizenship, fantasies which also overrepresent gender dynamics and sexuality; or, immigrants are further criminalized for their irresponsible attachment to the benefits of freedom, without the work or in the extreme informality of kinds of work. Pete Wilson's speech, included here, reflects the simultaneous criminalization of immigrants using the rhetoric of self-responsibility, as well as women's disciplining into assemblages that codify maternity as genre. The narrative genre becomes a human genre, imposing on bodies the politics of narrative purpose confined to dominant modes of reception.

Form mediates the present and the futurial, while precedent whispers between the margins but *takes hold* in the forms and arrangements inscribed. Precedent: that is, history. But let's understand it differently, as juridical. That is, *de jure* personhoods in the world of events that are not phenomena or spectacular/spectral. What works in poetics is the preservation that is not phenomenal but language, form that is in the world as both precedent to knowledge and futurial arrangements of its articulations.

precis is the being-aware of always-being in a position of putting meaning back into the world.

josé felipe alvergue was born in San Salvador, El Salvador, and grew up on the Mexico/US border. He is a graduate of both the Buffalo Poetics and CalArts Writing programs. As a grain of the Central American diaspora he works between text, performance, and archive in mapping the transnationalisms that shape residential identity. josé also teaches transnational and contemporary literature in Wisconsin, and is the author of *gist : rift : drift : bloom* (Further Other Book Works, 2015).

Offset printed in the United States
by Edwards Brothers Malloy, Ann Arbor, Michigan
On 55# Glatfelter B18 Antique
Acid Free Archival Quality Recycled Paper

Library of Congress Cataloging-in-Publication Data

Names: Alvergue, José Felipe, author.
Title: Precis / José Felipe Alvergue.
Description: Oakland, Califorina : Omnidawn Publishing, [2017]
Identifiers: LCCN 2016045484 | ISBN 9781632430304 (pbk. : alk. paper)
Classification: LCC PS3601.L879 A6 2017 | DDC 811/.6--dc23
LC record available at https://lccn.loc.gov/2016045484

Published by Omnidawn Publishing, Oakland, California
www.omnidawn.com (510) 237-5472 (800) 792-4957
10 9 8 7 6 5 4 3 2 1
ISBN: 978-1-63243-030-4

Publication of this book was made possible in part by gifts from:
The New Place Fund
Robin & Curt Caton

Rusty Morrison & Ken Keegan, senior editors & co-publishers
Gillian Olivia Blythe Hamel, managing editor
Cassandra Smith, poetry editor & book designer
Sharon Zetter, poetry editor, book designer & development officer
Liza Flum, poetry editor & marketing assistant
Peter Burghardt, poetry editor
Juliana Paslay, fiction editor
Gail Aronson, fiction editor
Cameron Stuart, marketing assistant
Avren Keating, administrative assistant
Kevin Peters, *OmniVerse* Lit Scene editor
Sara Burant, *OmniVerse* reviews editor
Josie Gallup, publicity assistant
SD Sumner, copyeditor
Briana Swain, marketing assistant